The Death of Protestant Theology: Apocrypha

ISBN 979-8-234-05245-2

Published by Jacob Anglin
relict9@gmail.com

The Death of Protestant Theology: Apocrypha

Dan David Elihu

Dante has his *Divine Comedy*, Lewis has Aslan, and yet we wonder only over *The Screwtape Letters*, while yet scorning in silence *The Great Divorce* and *Till We Have Faces*. I have this, my *Apocrypha*, a word we Protestants use to say but one thing: "It is not scripture." And a word the church knows to mean another: "Saints wrote this for study, let it be read." I wrote this for study; I wrote this out of study. Jack hated the feelings of sin and sawdust it took to write as a devil, and now any boy may pray himself to sleep and laugh at the devil's temptation. Dante ridiculed the world for being evil, the church for being of the world, and yet remembered fondly all he loved, from poet to dead friend. And how fondly we remember and praise Dante. I therefore, as all great authors before me, stand by every word I write. Yet be warned that I wrote as a man tasked with telling only the truth. I wish to be hated for my failure, to boldly expose every crack and each crease in my faith. Either this cloak is a precious gift, as Joseph's, which shall be slathered in blood by wolves, or this is all worthless, and one would do well to read Paul. But, if Paul, one must also read Peter. And if Peter, James. Of course, what is James without the advice of John, who had greater faith even than he? But what are these men apart from the record of them given by Luke? And who is the gentile Luke without Christ? Yet Christ came to fulfill the Law and the Prophets in accordance with the Writings. Therefore, how can you condemn me for writing as the writers of the epistles wrote, unless you learn the epistles, written out of the gospels, written out of the word of God from Genesis to the Prophets, all ending in Revelation, John's Apocalypse, for the writing of which he was denied death and being united with his beloved friend and king? Yes, James died first, and John was tasked to die last, living without brother and without his God. I know my faith is true, but you do not. You cannot say "yes" or "no," for you have refused the study of scripture. I did not write this to be read. I wrote this, drinking coffee as I read the epistles, having studied all scripture time and again, compelled to know, "had I been asked … would I falter?" I have yet to understand what I was asked and why, yet this I know well: I have done as my beloved desires; I have told the truth and held saints to his standard, and his alone. These, therefore, are open letters, written for any who wish to know, "How well do I know the Bible?" And the answer, no matter how many times you read these six essays, will prove to be, each and every time: "Not well enough." I only ask, then, that you read and read and read again the word of God, and that each time you happen upon this volume on your shelf, you remember you were told to study the word of God and go and do as you were told, until you can read this without guilt at having neglected your faith, at having neglected my God, who died for the sins of the whole world—if only the world would stop and listen. And one final note, as I know it will come up: This writing style, the open letter, the written sermon, the religious essay, the epistle, is a legacy of the church into history. This is a polite way of saying that thinkers, theologians, and saints throughout our history have written epistles, the style, without any thinking they were writing scripture. The issue is, to be blunt, that you Protestants read much less than you claim to, and therefore know very little about history. But yes, I quote scripture, speak theology, rebuke men, praise God, and write without doubt or hesitation that if I were wrong, I would be without excuse, and if I am right, I have made my point all the more sincerely. This is an expression of my faith, this is a challenge of my faith, this is a deed done as a sacrifice for my Lord, this is something I am rather proud of, as no one else has bothered to stop and say, "We were supposed to listen to him, you know; he warned us we would get rather lax about all this." And now someone has, and that rather brings me joy.

Regards,
Dan David Elihu

p.s. For two weeks now, the devil—my adversary—has tormented me: ill health, sleepless nights, demonic visions, dialogs, and all prayers left unanswered. I have begged and demanded for death. Worse, my mind, even my flesh, is not my own, but this roommate seeks to gnaw at my bones. I cannot chew, for he chops as a mule. I cannot sit, for he squirms as a python. I cannot relax, for he is only malice, a rage as black as to be androgynous. I am allowed music, but he hears only the noise used to block out his own discord. In this alone he, seeking to escape, fails, and my ears are allowed some harmony, although when I wish to sing, he is out of tune, as Nero. Even now I do not write, although I do, but a sledgehammer tied to a clenched fist fidgets away from these words. "Who knows," I feel him hopelessly lie, "He may decide against writing against me and for God Christ; I may strike his body again." I have dialoged against Ahavel before—I say his name to him with the patience of a loving father, and his iced-over hatred, black as Cain, assures me again he is no mere fallen angel, but the lowest angel. Two weeks. Yes, for two weeks I have worn a rosary and refused to take it off. So I am handed over to the devil as Christ and Job. Know this: the Devil hates no other alive more than I. And there is none righteous alive greater than I. And the devil hates me, this hate my only prize. The enemy sent a thorn in the side of St. Paul. Thus, a choice is made for me. Have you enticed demonic hate? Have you endured the devil, being steadfast, as asked by St. Peter? Have you been mocked, "Friend of Christ, servant of God, one who believes Jesus will be the everlasting father, thus believing the servant Isaiah"? Has the adversary broken your pen for writing against him? Oh, how he would love to slit my throat, but my life alone is Christ's. Have you been denied sleep for faith? Have you fasted and witnessed? And this is the worst of it: he hates each moment torturing more than I. But when has hate stopped the devil from tempting God to sin in the false hope God would thus break his promise by which all sinners are condemned to hell? And yet, even given two years of torment, one year of sickness, and two weeks of Judas's possession, I have yet to sin. Yes, the Lord spoke, "You have equipped the last of the armor of God." And now I live as one who knows too much of heaven. Water is dead; in New Narnia it will be alive.

I Dan

CHAPTER 1

1To the church, and churches, and the saints without the body, in light of the present schisms: Grace has been obscured and peace denied. Greetings. 2And here is how peace is achieved, having been hard-pressed—each convicted by his own spirit having accepted and received the laying on of fire—let each member turn itself to the head. 3What I say is twofold. For first the heart is hard for the sake of the denial of the Spirit, leaving the outside washed and all within, in speech, or in illness, or in ailment and injury, a salt-water cistern. And so the church, being Christ's body—and if his body, he has also entrusted us with the heart, who gives us all comfort—is broken by heresy. 4For, denying the Holy Spirit, we breed heresies; denying harmony, we hasten the leaven. And if heresy, our faith is without love, and without love there are no works of faith, and working without faith were born schisms, and hidden in schisms the impulse to grasp the sword. 5But we were called to submission to the head who sends his blood to the body by the heart. 6Therefore, this saying is true: "Fickle is the Spirit, who desires our will and is favored by those who favor the head." 7For the head says, "Run!" and the heart hastens. 8The Lord commands, "Rest!" and the blood grows thin in weakness. 9And the heart bleeds passion, the eyes telling of a virgin in distress. Yet you take with the hand, even as the Spirit aids you in seeking out the weak to feed. Instead, you grow fat at his love feast, and in the face of your apostasy the Spirit leaves the house empty and swept for the devil to claim. 10And how have we come to this in the face of our God's assurance? How readily has the body forsaken the head? 11For the apostles forewarned, "They shall come to divide us," just as the elders warned us beforehand, "Do not eat with them, nor should the lady allow any of their perdition into her house, lest they be accepted by her reputation." 12Yet we have elevated men of great learning, men of the house of the Pharisee and the heretic, the gnostic and the Judaizer, the lost of the world and the lost born into our own temples. 13And if any of these are divided, then all are divided by the house of Satan. 14For a house divided against itself shall not stand, but our house has one foundation, who is Christ, and two pillars, which are baptism—that all might be brought to the table—and the eucharist—that all might remain pure in his house. [15]Yet we have made a mockery of his will and harmony, for, "The multitudes of your sacrifices—what are they to me? I will not listen. Your hands are full of blood." [16]In times past, this was only the blood of the innocent—but none are innocent—and of lambs. But in these last days, in your unending rebellion—for the gates of hades cannot overcome—we are guilty of profaning the blood of the Lamb who was slain.

Chapter 2

[1]Was not the promise for you, and your children, and for all who were afar off? [2]But now I say to the bride, "The promise is for the saints, and your children, but you are all afar off." [3]For you forsook all, and all, as one, must come again to God, [4]now cleansed in faith, that your unrighteous blasphemy and profane deeds may be forgiven by the Lamb of God, who was God and is our God, being the Son of God made manifest as the word of God, to whom the bulk of the scriptures testify. [5]For this is the first, and the last, and from time before all time was his will, that we sabbath toward his sacrifice in all faith and righteous deeds. [6]And here another cry against the church is found. [7]For without faithful guard through the night, as her sisters before in the days of Eden's shadow, and of Babel's destruction, and of the Egyptian desert, and of Ephraim's destruction and Jerusalem's judgment, our church has turned harlot, herself splintered into five virgins without oil. [8]Yet from out of the five shall five be found in all hope on this hill, shining bright in all faith, [9]daughters who on that last day shall be clothed in all glory, as our Lord shall forget the works of the five who fell away. [10]Yes, our one church of a thousand schisms—from neck to scattered toe, as God alone is our head—has given herself over to manifold idolatries born in our own hearts, in denial of Christ's heart. [11]But there is only one idolatry, which is money, and pride, being the way of rebellion. Yes, the way of the prince of the power of the air who yet prowls in seeking to leaven the body. [12]This one we give many names. Indeed, each sinner saved gives his idol a new name. She is fashioned in the saint's image as shown unto the sinner in the mirror of baptism, with the promise, "Obey and be a son of God." [13]Yet we also fashion our idol in our own image, [14]and the betrothed sets her image upon the throne of God. Yes, our condemnation is just. [15]Now he who has ears let him hear: "We each fashion an idol in our image. We each name our idol 'son of God.' We each shape our idol after the Spirit, denying the Spirit who is God." [16]We know this throne is to be eternally ceded to Christ. But instead, you desire your new heart to be as the old. [17]The heart of stone was fed by your own pride.

Chapter 3

1Do you not know the Father's pride is love? 2And all are to love, denying their own pride just as the Son of Man, who was condemned by our pride, died that we might live. 3And now, dead to this pride and risen, in Christ, through love of the Father's pride, who is Jesus Christ our Lord, we are slaves to God's pride. Amen. 4And thus, our groom cried, "Forgive them, they know not what they are doing." 5But you, now knowing, each week being reminded what you are doing, idolizing even his cross, continue in sin! 6You blaspheme in speech! You profane his witness in deed! You hold grudges against brothers! You refuse forgiveness, yourselves forgiven! 7You each exalt your salvation rather than your Savior, 8renouncing the salvation of lost sheep and sons wandering in the mud, when you were called to welcome lost brothers and save strangers from stumbling. 9But go, continue, and your reward—so jealously neglected—shall be as lost as Saul and Jonah, 10and shall be given instead to the sons of David in humility, and the sons of Nineveh in righteousness who, left in sin each day Jonah delayed, repented in faith after piercing rebuke. 11And is this not your rebuke? 12But on the last day, cry, "Lord, Lord," 13for your reward will be lost and given over to the righteous robed in wedding clothes. 14And as Judas and Ananias you were redeemed, and as Iscariot and Sapphira you seek to deny the Spirit of redemption. 15It is not in vain we are warned, "Christ shall not be twice crucified." Therefore, repent, lest you be found twice dead. 16But we are called to earn the favor of our gracious Father 17for the sake of our love for Christ Jesus, who, dying in our place, commands we die also to our own sin. 18And who, suffering before the lost, commands that we who were once lost endure patiently the suffering born of rebellion—both ours and that of the world we preach peace to.

Chapter 4

1And it is in this way, according to the gospel, that we are to be known by each other, by the heretic, and by the world. A light in the dark, a lamp on a hill, an elder at the gate. 2And should we stumble, as Lot before us, the Lord shall send a messenger that we might, for the sake of our righteous reputation—but if righteous, Christ's—overcome in the service of our Father who foreknew us. 3And, foreknowing, who sent Christ into the world, as so many deny, giving all those known to the Father over to Christ—oh, how often the saints deeds deny—and leaving all apart from the Father without Christ. 4For being apart from the Spirit, all blaspheme against the work of God in our conscience, which convicts even the pagan toward the Father's will, that all in sheol and on the earth might live or die at the foot of the singular throne of God, given unto the man Jesus of Nazareth, who is Christ. [5]But I strive to keep my conscience clear before the God of St. Paul's fathers and before man such as those St. Paul confessed, "I follow the way," as my God knew a remnant, as in the day of Noah, would receive the Son, [6]such that it is asked in truth by the Son, "But when I return, shall I find faith on this earth?" [7]And, as the Father's love commands, "Every knee shall bow, and every tongue confess." [8]Not for the love of this world, but for the sake of the elect who take up their cross, who place both hands on the plow, and who follow Christ even if Mammon should threaten to provide their daily bread. [9]But this is the way of faith, not that we stand, but that we rise. [10]Not that we are Christ, but that we attest to our brother, who asked for our adoption, our God who married through his death our death into his life, as he and the Father ordained from the beginning. [11]For it was not in vain that Christ said of himself, "He will crush your head, and you will strike his heel." [12]And of his sons, "So God created man in his own image, in the image of God he created him; male and female he created them." [13]And if in his image, and if male and female, and if the seed of the woman is to remain the Son of God in whose image man was created, being fashioned by his hands, then all are Christ's, given over to our King according to the Father who gave to each soul the breath of life. [14]This is the love and mercy of our God, [15]the Father of Obed-Edom and the Centurion, of the Babylonian and the Syrian, of Manasseh the son of David, and of all else who remain steadfast, [16]having been converted as Paul to this way, the way to our Father, jealously guarded by the angels set under authority, being placed under Christ who is above the angels. [17]And this is our testimony, that Christ died for the whole world. Yet we refuse the world this message. [18]Yes, refusing even to agree on the foundation, building with foreign stones, known to our fathers, in rebellion against the saints we call foreign for the sin of having built according to their fathers. [19]We deny the harmony of Christ, [20]denying the one church, refusing the eucharist to the baptized, refusing to baptize households, refusing to honor the liturgy, and changing the liturgy only to deepen our schisms. [21]Or did our Lord not read aloud the word of God to the congregation of the synagogue of his people according to the common tongue? [22]Yes, and the brazen serpent spoke the scriptures carved in the bronze tongue as Daniel preached in the tongue of gold, preaching the end of the gentiles' age, [23]that all peoples, and kings, and nations would hear the cry of the Lord, "Repent and be baptized," given first to John and kept even by the disciple Christ loved.

Chapter 5

[1]Is this not the way of Christ, of the great speaker, of Paul, of Cephas? [2]Yet Paul condemned Peter at Antioch for inaugurating a schism. [3]Therefore, I shall condemn Peter also: "You are in sin, and refuse to lift a finger to lighten the load you have given." [4]Do not gloat! Or did James and Barnabas not fall into schism in their own hearts? [5]We are called to feed the widow, love the Samaritan, and forgive the tax collector. And how far we have fallen! [6]Therefore, as Paul was, all are called to rebuke their brother, as the son of Pharisees rebuked even the Jews, he of the one chosen people condemning his own chosen people, [7]you are to know the church is called to condemn the church. [8]To the churches, rebuke first your churches. [9]To the saints without the body, seek out the blood, and when denied move on; and finding the blood, first learn in silence, then speak as called by God. [10]For there is one baptism, one body, one resurrection, one God, and one Messiah who was sent to die before all as one witness, as attested by the Holy Spirit who quickened the hearts of the prophets and apostles. [11]Yet we are many and our sins are manifold. [12]Where we see many, God sees one embroiled in schism. [13]The world sees fools, yet the devil sees a sickly bride. [14]The Spirit says to each in his own heart, "Walk the way in harmony," [15]yet the many refuse the one who calls, "Be one as Christ is one." [16]In this way all have fallen short of the glory of God. [17]And all having fallen, all have grown proud—when each should be in mourning. [18]There is no soundness from east to west, [19]just as in times past God's chosen found no righteous saints from Judah to the north; [20]instead, their Lord condemned Israel to judgment. [21]Shall we not also be judged for our deeds on last day, [22]the few having increased the harvest as others squandered their inheritance? But even then our Lord will condemn pride foremost in judgment, [23]sparing the hopeful who forgive the fate of their elder brothers, whose deeds were worked only for greater wages, unaware that all are to be friends of God. [24]Therefore, if you are not in harmony with his Spirit now, how shall you receive his harmony in heaven?

Chapter 6

[1]Were you shrewd managers in the world? Then having died to self, serve Christ. [2]Or did you serve for others who sin? Then serve better he who died for all sinners. [3]And having begun in the wisdom of the world, finish now in the innocence of the Spirit. [4]You who are apart from wisdom—in the world and of Christ—do you, being foolish, believe you are wise? [5]For it is foolish to serve in Christ's name, serving the saints, in place of serving for status in the world, when you failed in your sin to ever meet even the godless standards of

the world. [6]And to then believe, having been rejected by the world for your sloth, that you would be made righteous in sloth by squandering the resources of the body, is to profane God. [7]But having failed to serve well, serving only in appearance, proximity to the body is nowise a sign of faith, nor of the innocence of doves. [8]For it is well said that the gospel reveals a righteousness which is by faith from faith, from first to last. [9]In this way it is declared that righteousness can never be faith, [10]but in faith the saints are free to pursue righteousness—and none are righteous apart from Christ, [11]as the Spirit guides all in right works, those spiritual deeds done before the Lord for sake of the love of our Father [12]who graciously sacrificed his son that Christ might take the freed saints as his own body. [13]Or had Christ not loved the world, would the Father have given the life of all life as the price for sinners' sin and death? [14]But loving all as our Father loves all, Jesus the king of Israel and the son of Abraham died for his children, [15]having created all according to the will of God as established at the beginning. [16]I fear the love of the Father for the eternally begotten is yet too wonderful for you who quarrel and refuse solid food. [17]The meat has perished, and it stinks. [18]Even the milk is spoiled, and this is no surprise. [19]For, as a prisoner of the Lord, an apostle saw none were worthy of the calling he received, [20]pleading—for what are the epistles but faithful pleas?—"I urge you to live a life worthy of the calling you received." [21]But none were faithful before the pain of prison, rejection, starvation, and the thorn in the side, the demonic messengers, [22]but instead they hid as you now hide, saying—hidden in your heart where only he may hear—"The angels ignore me, for I never threaten their thrones in the church. Let the head cleanse his own body as before. Who called that I am to rebuke heresy?" [23]And yet Judas the brother of Christ said unto us, "There will be men who divide you and do not have the spirit." [24]You who refuse to discern—as your fathers before you—are without excuse. [25]Refusing the head's call of rebuke, you are unworthy of the revival you have refused.

Chapter 7

[1]Their condemnation was just. Now also shall ours be, [2]for we were set free and have let thieves into the temple. [3]We were redeemed and have given the body to demons. [4]You were loved and have denied your lover. For you, in your deeds, denied Christ. [5]But he wishes better things for you, [6]and where sin abounds, grace abounds also. [7]And how gracious the words, "Lord, remember me when you enter your kingdom." [8]Seeing Christ, even having forsaken salvation, that faithful confession the act of loving a righteous man unloved. [9]And knowing only that he was first loved, without the promise of new life, the thief loved the servant who

is our King. [10]And where is such love as this? [11]Who has given all to God? [12]As for myself, my heart bleeds for Christ. [13]But this is his word, that he shall judge our deeds, [14]as he loved the thief whose one deed was etched into eternity, our Lord eternally cherishing: "Remember me." [15]It is in this way we are to cherish the love of our Lord for those who love the Lord, [16]the Spirit cherishing brothers of God according to the will of the Father. [17]Therefore, in the pursuit of a righteousness greater than that of the Pharisees, of a faith which endures all trials, an assurance which increases all hope, and the steadfast adherence to the way of Jesus Christ, all are found wanting. [18]How few have housed angels, how few have fed the children, and who has offered water to true saints? [19]Instead, each fattens the goats, kneads leaven into the church, and causes the children to stumble by excusing shared sins. [20]"Here is our favored station, now come, give your alms, which are many, to the saints. [21]We are broken as you, yet together we are in harmony, guilty before our God for unknown sins." [22]But let us show that there you will find all promise of salvation is for naught. [23]"When a wicked man dies, his hope perishes; all he expected from his power comes to nothing." [24]If this is the unveiling of sin in death, then lo, our unveiling unto life comes also only on the day our hope is fulfilled, [25]should we until that day, through suffering, hope in Christ and never seek the comforts of this life ruled by the arm of the oppressor. [26]But as Christ died and rose again, let us suffer in Christ that all may know the righteousness of the God who gives daily bread to the oppressed.

Chapter 8

[1]Therefore, you are warned that the enemies of God seek to purchase your hope, purchasing simultaneously the opportunity to partake with you of death. [2]Or do you not recall, "Such men are false apostles, deceitful workmen, masquerading as apostles of Christ. [3]And no wonder, for Satan himself masquerades as an angel of light. [4]It is not surprising, then, if his servants masquerade as servants of righteousness. Their end will be what their actions deserve." [5]For they say in their hearts, "The Spirit ignores us; he must nowise speak. [6]The Spirit is silent; I must tell a tale of his speaking. [7]The Spirit draws me back to an unrepented sin, kept hidden; I shall obey eventually and feel guilty each day. I seek out God's will, yet he remembers yesterday and ignores my desire for the future. [8]Yes, God is distant. I do right deeds, and I have witnesses who assure me of my right ways, and everywhere I go my gospel is preached, for I in my guilt preach continually. [9]However, I am without fear, for, 'He will command his angels concerning you to guard you carefully; they will lift you up in their hands, so that you will not strike your

foot on a stone.' [10]And now in my time of trial I shall confess this comfort of scripture, which came to me in the night, the fruit of the Spirit's conviction, which now fades away. [11]But still each day I seek only to be assured that I am a servant of righteousness, so let God aid my masquerade." [12]Yes, as Christ warned, such is the heart of the leaven. [13]As Paul preached, such are the birds in our branches. [14]And as Peter, Jacob, and Jude warned and forewarned, such are those twice dead, hiding in shifting shadow. [15]Know that in Christ is no shifting shadow, in the Father only bright light, [16]yet the Spirit, who is all light, is quenched by his own body, so that his light shall not expose their hidden idols. Godless apostates; faithless saints. [17]These hearts of stone are trapped in faithless denial of Christ's cleansing love. [18]And the wheat, choked in worries, courts the tares, crying, "Peace, peace," that the goats and the Pharisees would remain, and with them their alms and tithes, numbers and conviction, labor and aid, such that in fear of man and love of money your faith would be supplanted, a faith which is to be in the aid and conviction of the Spirit, who rebukes you as the twice dead will not. [19]Nor would the faithless seek ever to offend your pride, which covers over their own sin. [20]But we are called to discern—in harmony, according to the harmony given to the souls continually in prayer.

Chapter 9

[1]Yes, in word and deed and suffering, if only as one called, I work that all may know the hope of salvation, squandered by all given already to this hope, just as Jerusalem squandered it before. [2]I am grieved as Paul was, and I pray over you as Christ did over Jerusalem. [3]Yet you pray only in fits and starts, for your own heart, never giving your desire over to the Spirit in Christ. [4]You pray not to discern, but for your own gain. [5]Now I command you to pray that you would lose yourself in Jesus our Lord, to be given over to the Spirit who guides the new heart, saving your temple—your own body—which is now Christ's bride. [6]Or do my rebukes offend you sons of Cephas, Paul, Apollos, and even Christ? [7]Or are you as righteous as Moses, who condemned brothers to death in rebuking Israel? [8]Are you pure as Stephen, who was stoned for rebuking his religious leaders? [9]For I now rebuke the body and her heads, who have become the devil's tails. [10]Is this not Christ? Was this not Paul? For even now my soul, as with the souls of the few who seek also to imitate Christ, cries out against the saints. [11]But say in your heart, "Who are you to convict my soul?" For wisdom is tested by the ear, and conviction is born of the Spirit. To know in faith "I am convicted" is to know—and shudder—that "Christ stands in my way." [12]Yet Saul repented before Christ as Hezekiah pled for mercy. [13]But are you in your own conviction

above your fellow workers, too righteous to plea for forgiveness? [14]I know well how Christ was too righteous to plead forgiveness for himself, in faith righteously being nailed to the cross for your sins instead. Are not our convictions just? [15]For in faith many righteous men were called for their bride, like both David and Othniel slaying foes for the sake of the Lord's people, and of his people a bride, that they may be rewarded in accord with their faithful deeds. [16]Yet Christ's reward was suffering, and in exchange for all life he was handed over to death, that Job might never boast, and that the martyrs might be given robes of glory. [17]Now it is you who are called to suffer for your bride, the bride of Christ, and will you refuse this call? [18]And having refused your call will you blaspheme his Spirit? [19]Or will you begin in faith and fall away that you may say, "I began the tower, but I was given only a mina?" [20]Did Christ leave the foundation incomplete? Then having been brought into his house, who are you to refuse the call, taking his blood, only to leave his work, which is now your work, incomplete? [21]For Christ shall prevail, as Mordecai well knew, exhorting Esther to risk all, without conviction by the Holy Spirit, but only by faith and reason, that they might serve rightly their Lord who promised our father Abraham the stars in the sky. [22]And this is the legacy of the saints, of the faithful, of the sons of God, of the brothers of Jesus Christ; but is it the legacy you shall leave? [23]For the remnant is few, the harvest is plentiful, and uncountable are the tares. [24]Did not Christ seek a nation prepared for the Messiah by revelation? Yet he found only seventy worthy of carrying out his ministry. Are even seventy of such reputation known among the saints of this day? How much less so you who refuse conviction, you who wrestle doubt in denial of the God who denies all doubt as double-minded?

Chapter 10

[1]For he was made flesh, carved into stone hearts through death, that all would be without excuse. [2]And what then is your excuse, you wicked and faithless congregation? [3]For first were the earliest saints, from John's Baptism to the Resurrection, and all preaching and teaching, healing and feeding, debating and loving ministry in between. [4]Then, Christ risen into heaven, came the first additions, brought in through the preaching of Peter and the tongues of Pentecost. [5]And how many endured the sufferings of scattering and persecutions as the way was spread by the few in faith throughout all the places of worship of the people of God, and among the great cities of the empire who ruled over the world, [6]preaching peace and grace, Christ and obedience—obedience to God and man—that all would know God? [7]And yet even from the beginning, with Paul and the twelve as witnesses, and

the deaths of Iscariot and Ananias as warnings, we were left a legacy of cautions and rebukes. [8]How often did Paul demand that his sons in faith be given heed by those he loved as sons? [9]In the same way we find that Jude and John rebuked heretics in their midst. For Paul uncovered rebellion against all right preaching, ever spreading in the wake of his absence. [10]Thus we know it was true of the first church, from the first day, as it is true now, and was true in every age of schism, schisms, and scattering, that "none are righteous, no, not even one." [11]And our history is a history of rebellion, of rebuke, and of failure. For it is said in faith, "To whom our fathers would not obey, but thrust Christ's apostles from them, and their hearts turned to the world." [12]Such was the day of the Holy Spirit: "You stiff-necked and uncircumcised in heart and ears, you resist the Holy Spirit as your fathers did. Which of the prophets and apostles did we not resist, seeking freedom from sin without the conviction born in deification? [13]But we have ever abandoned the church to thieves and murderers. For the church received the word by the disposition of the Word of God and has not kept it." [14]Or do I lie? For these words were first spoken by the saints unto the people of God. And now I, a saint, speak these words anew unto fellow saints. [15]Do I sin? But what did Christ preach to his own people, as all are also now his people, saying, "And you say, 'if we had lived in the days of our forefathers, we would not have taken part with them in shedding the blood of the prophets.' [16]So you testify against yourselves that you are the descendants of those who murdered the prophets." [17]Or are we not all the descendants of the one body? [18]"You snakes! You brood of vipers! How will you escape being condemned to hell?" [19]But night is yet to come, and this day is the same day as Pentecost. Are you therefore more righteous than the church, which abandoned the gospel for a new gospel, which is no gospel at all? Are you more righteous than the church, which paid to be taught by heretics what Paul offered free of charge? Are you more righteous than the lust and gluttony and blasphemy of the Corinthians? [20]Or are you pure in you adherence to theology, and right in your generations, just as the Hebrews who were condemned rightly by Paul when he said, "But Christ is faithful as a son over God's house. And we are his house, if we hold on to our courage." [21]If you are so righteous, do you remain steadfast? If you are right before God, do you keep your courage? If you, and your members, are right before God, do you as a body obey? But only if. [22]"And to whom did God swear that they would never enter his rest if not to those who disobeyed? [23]So we see that they were not able to enter because of their unbelief. [24]Therefore, since the promise of entering his rest still stands, let us be careful that none of you be found to have fallen short." [25]For these warnings, and all rebukes, are given to those with ears to hear, to be read in the assembly of the saints. [26]Are we as saints more righteous than the saints educated by Paul and Titus and James, and the few even by Christ? Then these condemnations stand in scripture as all scripture stands in Christ.

Chapter 11

[1]And this I know: "Whoever is not with me is against me, whoever does not gather for me scatters, but anyone who gives you a cup of water in my name because you belong to the Messiah will certainly not lose their reward." [2]Thus, I pray this water may refresh your soul in our Lord's name. [3]And now I warn. Warning of the end. Warning of damnation. Warning of unrepented sin. And warning all of Christ's violent return against the world, and all saints found in the world, apart from the Spirit. [4]I warn his church, myself knowing, teaching, and preaching in the way of his first coming, his final death and resurrection. [5]Yes, I have warned all, and none give ear. [6]Forgiving all, I find that none sought grace. [7]Working for all saints, I find they wish I would wash their feet, which have never walked the way. I wash the sandals of hired hands. [8]All is pain. All is torment. The enemy seeks to devour every day. [9]Yet my body does not break with labor, nor my soul with hopelessness, [10]for I am fed my daily bread each day we march on through the wilderness, foreigners through those hopeless lands. [11]I praised God each day, and all refused ear; I served God through the night, and the body dreamed slothful dreams—dreaming that they may yet sin. [12]And sin they shall, for his patience is his wrath. [13]It would seem I suffer for naught. It would appear that the church has failed. It would look as though there will be no faith—no, none at all—upon this earth when our King returns. [14]For I do not write to the lost, nor into the dark, but I light the lamps, I cry out at the city gate, I cast fresh salt into vain salt flats, I teach healing to worthless physicians. [15]And I am alone among the saints, yet none are above Christ. [16]And in serving Christ Jesus I am beneath you, that you may be washed.

Chapter 12

[1]I pray to be free of you soon, safe in my Lord's arms. [2]Yet to live is Christ, and Christ is dying, for the body is dead. [3]And the body shall stink like Lazareth when the trumpet calls and the remnant left pure are lifted up, [4]but the many remain, of every fold of our one body, to ride the beast. [5]Abraham died for nothing. Moses served fools for forty years. Noah suffered to spare our godless people. Adam fell for none to call out for the promised Savior. David was tested for a throne over a nation unworthy of their king. Finally, Jesus our

King suffered and died for a world disin-
terested in truth. "And what are works in
keeping with eternal life?" 6For we are the
harlot, one shattered, headless, heretical,
leprous church. 7And still, we remain his
church until he calls us home. 8Beloved,
forgive your debtors; this I warn. 9As for
myself, I shall live in Christ and pray every
day to receive from out of my Father's
Spirit—given in the elevation of God
above Godhead—the gain of salvation,
the only hope I hope in all faith. 10And
having been bid by Christ Jesus our God
according to the Father's Spirit to record
this, and these, and all things unveiled
by my speaking, as all before were called
yet all refused, I alone in faith write this
plea, that in this last age all are without
excuse. 11Judge, beloved, my God is He!
12If anyone does not love the Lord, let that
person be cursed. 13Come, Lord!

Chapter 13

1Serve Christ until his return. Remain
steadfast that we would hasten his return.
Honor God that you would be found
without blemish in this wicked church
of schisms. Remain in Christ that your
brothers would be without excuse. Love
Jesus, exposing hired hands. 2And pray
continually, that the Spirit might rule
the flesh, the heart, and the head, as Jesus
remained always in the Holy Spirit, having
begun the church by his baptism. 3All sin,
yet by righteous prayer Peter was saved.
All saints pray, yet without fervent prayer
James was beheaded. John was righteous,
warning of the end, yet he lived a life
apart from the brother who loved him in
adoption and outlived the brother who
worked with Him in Christ, John's reward
for his righteousness being long suffering
for this hope we have received. 4For by
Christ all are sons of God, just as the angels
are. 5And as a son of God, Lucifer, called
Ahavel, fell away, his name blotted out,
yet all know, as testified through John,
"God is love." 6Now then, your adulteries
are forgiven. 7Go and praise the Lord's
table, knowing that "I will establish my
covenant with you: Never again will all
life be destroyed by the waters of a flood;
never again will there be a flood to destroy
the earth." 8But the Lamb will return by
blood and by fire, and having cleared his
threshing floor, "seedtime and harvest,
cold and heat, summer and winter, day
and night will never cease." 9Nor will the
ground be any longer cursed, but "the
one who fails to reach a hundred will
be considered accursed." 10Then, after a
thousand years, the sands of the sea shall
turn against Jerusalem, and the earth shall
no longer endure. 11For this is apocrypha;
know that Revelation is the beginning of
history. 12My love to all of you in Jesus
Christ. Amen.

II Dan

Chapter 1

1Dan David, a watchman bid watch over the woman who will ride the beast, 2to the few who will hear the trumpet call, the fewer hairs who will be lifted out from this fate, 3in light of the gospel recorded in an orderly fashion by the saints, 4that all may be without excuse; greetings. 5I strive in all I do to draw out of the Holy Ghost words of scripture, 6that all may find again the witness given already by our God in the hope that the faithless may still understand, and that the gnostic will be frustrated should any venture to venerate my writings. 7Now I must warn all with only my wisdom given of the Spirit who is God, hoping the hearer of faith aligns in Christ Jesus by righteous deeds inspired by the spiritual insight given to all in right prayer, 8that they may grow in theosis, wearing the armor of God unto completion. 9Lord, I pray this work hastens the hearer toward the deeds of return. Amen. 10I know you are all cowards. 11Having sacrificed everything to begin, losing all you had, you fear sacrificing anything you have left. 12And knowing you must give all again to him at the start of each day, you ignore God long into the restless night. 13You are all proud; you have pride about the clothes for your labors and your daily bread, and all are food for the moths. 14But only kill this pride in prayer, and sacrifice the worthless things of this world. 15Wealth, use for God; 16friends, give to God; 17fellow Christians, pray and rebuke in faith; 18reputation, guard in right deeds; 19as for your good name, abandon it to be called instead fools by your church, yes, even by your own congregation. 20For there is much work and little reward should you serve Christ in this godless life. 21But you each claim already to serve our Lord. You do not. 22Thus, when you pray, he reminds you of unrepented sin, ignoring you. 23You have taken God's name in vain, and he leaves you in your torment. "Am I saved?" you ask. Do you not know God answers gladly, "Yes," when you are righteous in faithful deeds and clear in conscience? 24God's silence is your rebuke. 25Now I am done with cowardice. 26You all love the world. You all love the world. Yes, you all, even the hearer, love the world. 27Do you not know that to love your own life, to love this life we live, to do even this is to love the world? 28And that hating heathens, damning pagans, spiting rivals, refusing water to the lost, and lamenting your sufferings as an outsider at the hand of this godless world, are no virtues but the very pride of this life you scorn in your own hypocrisy? 29Being so arrogant, you refuse love to the lost, instead elevating elders who teach you to deny the lost who are in need of light. 30And where is Christ in this? 31These are blind guides. For you were called to see the lost and to know the way, teaching all. 32You refuse to remember that without God so were you, and apart from God so now are your elders who deny the Spirit, loving their honored seats in the congregation. Meeting each week to scorn the dying, instead you will die in hell for your godless pride—unless you repent. 33I am done with all those who scoff.

Chapter 2

1You are all ignorant. You do not understand the will of God; you refuse to understand the scriptures. 2Do as the faithful did, without proof, as God asks, even if your fellow saints should mock and scorn. 3Do what the righteous ones of old did, losing time and abandoning wealth to privately aid the saints in their poverty and the lost in their need. 4Do these things knowing you will be scorned by the Spirit if you refuse, knowing Christ watches over you, praying you obey the Father's will. 5What is it to you when they mock you in the congregation? Let the goats screech doubt, but go and feed widows. 6As for sin, hate the root of evil, praying against it—this is wisdom—7and no longer accuse Christ Jesus, who cast out demons, of keeping demons for his glory, 8but resist instead the gates of hell, lest you fall away. 9For had the saints proved faithful, had the lost not resisted in sin, none would suffer the wages of death, nor would the Spirit mourn your rebellions. But this he died for, as he promised at the beginning. 10And this is scripture explained; let us move on. 11For now, having submitted to scripture in prayer, being given one task—which is to love—you argue. 12Yes, you begin, and sliding away you begin again, ever starting, yet never striving to finish, that you may say you are on his path. 13But you must find and remain on the path to the Father before you can run. 14And it is no warfare in spirit but only spiritual fraud against the Holy Ghost to begin and begin again. 15Now wear the armor of God and endure for the prize, for inviting demons and harboring doubt-ruled brothers to weaken your own faith is your sin, never your justification. And none of these are, as some falsely claim, a test of God. 16Arrogant cowards; the servant is never greater than the master. 17And in your doubt, you are mere dogs, no soldiers in Christ. 18Have you done a deed? Did you claim a lost soul? This is a wonder. But did you not know our Lord gave up all to save all the Father handed over? Then continue to imitate Christ; the harvest plentiful, this work is yet to be complete. And not his, which is fulfilled, but yours, which he has entrusted unto you.

Chapter 3

[1]And now, having rebuked all sin, I
finish in earnest this plea. [2]In the love of
Christ, by the Father's Spirit, I welcome
all who are in the faith given to all who
love the purpose of our Lord. [3]And being
numbered among the saints, having
begun the race, now striving for Christ,
know your every breath is a blessing to
the Holy Spirit who shares with all this
breath of life, who tires of restraining the
deeds of the false ones. [4]Now this is your
task, taking up the armor, the gifts of the
Spirit, to discover the goats and wolves, to
aid the demon-oppressed, and to expose
those who are antichrist. [5]For already
you strive to aid prodigals in need, should
these things be found in you; now save
also the sheep by ending the oppression of
false saints in the congregation. For Peter
did not mourn Judas, nor did he hesitate
to damn Sapphira. [6]And knowing already
that God guides you, in the spirit of peace,
toward those weak in the gospel, march
now in this harmony of God to all those
in darkness hidden in the weakness of the
saints, which is their pride. [7]Being the
scent of death to those being saved, know
that all are either for Christ or against the
Father's Spirit, which is now the Spirit of
Christ for the sake of the elect, as attested
to by John. [8]And this is war, and the
soldiers are few, but the soldiers alone will
have been the harvest. [9]Now having been
instructed and welcomed gladly, having
been warned of the wages of war, even the
few fall away. [10]For fear of losing friend,
father, reputation, and the invitations of
the saints, they will choose the Christmas
table over Christ who gave willingly his
blood for our table, passing over our sins.
[11]You are those who remain. I am sorry.
Know that he will remember you in his
kingdom. Amen.

III Dan

Chapter 1

1I, Dan, forewarning the saints of this day, according to the Spirit of God—who is God, who all know—and by the teachings—which the church alone has received—of Jesus Christ, the Son of God, to the church of my nation, that of America, and then to all the church, and churches, and the saints without the body: grace and peace. 2Our modern church, though in every age the saints of the age were modern, has mistaken her forefathers for Christ our one teacher, and her boundary stones, which they have moved, for the will of our one Father God. 3This rebuke is true, as it was ever the warning to the Pharisees. 4How often the elder son was handed control of the estate in rebellion against the Father's love for the prodigal. "And as our fathers before we will not tolerate prodigals." Yet it was your fathers who protested outside the redemption feasts my Father held for my brothers in Christ who were forgiven their sins. 5You godless saints who isolate yourselves in sin, your denial of the will of our Father, yourselves fathers, has shown your hearts of stone. 6Neither those who reject the tax collector, nor those who excuse their greed, nor those who refuse sinners, nor any who praise sin, shall enter the kingdom of God. 7But all who, loving that they are loved, love the lost, with these I shall stand and sing, "Well done, our brothers in Christ, you friends of God, who were worthy of all praise." 8For what is the rejection of the congregation, as that of the synagogue before, when my friend our God shall say alone to us, "Well done, my good and faithful servant"? 9For I follow the way that you called heresy, so I worship the God of Joseph, God's father by the very will of God, believing all things written in the law and the prophets. 10And thus, when I follow the Messiah whom you denied, I read his word and that of his saints in accordance with the word of even his Father's saints handed over to him through death, having been kept alive by the resurrection. Amen. 11I would ask, then, and not I but Christ, that you refuse the Pharisee an honored seat at your dining table, instead inviting the sinners to break bread. 12For the Pharisees pray, "I thank God I am free of sexual immorality, although my lust is hid, of wealth, of theft, and of the sinners' dishonorable reputation," 13But the lost pray—for all sheep were once lost—"I know I am a sinner. Lord save me from all I do which I do not want to do, remember my cry, and teach me how to honor you." Instead, you deny all at the devil's table the hope of salvation. And such were some of you. But you were washed, and ask in love to wash others. 14Therefore, show to all the same love shown you. 15And now I ask, not Christ but I, a mere imitator of our one Lord, that you walk straight where there are lost sheep. 16I ask you to wash the mud off the sandals of prodigals, offer cloaks to lost daughters, give living water, and water, to adulterous widows, and show love to broken orphans, as all are orphaned apart from their Father. 17Have you not heard their call? Have you grown deaf to their screams? Do you refuse to heed the prayer of the dying? 18Or do they not sing, "We live once and we die, we lie together and die alone, we lease love and receive lust. Let us drink until the day, let us forget the night and her sins, this life is death. God, do we not die beautifully?" 19As for myself, may God strike me down should I ever refuse to love the lost, heed their call, and pray they receive the witness I bleed out of Christ. 20But you I have watched deny, ignore, refuse, and rebuke. My anger—no, for who am I?—the Father's wrath burns against you. And you call yourselves little Christs. You are reeds which break in the hand. 21Is today not the last day? Are we not called to live out suffering in Christ, knowing the day is short and to die is gain? 22For I am so called, but when I see your faith without deeds, it would seem you have not received such a call. Who am I to judge? 23But on the last day Christ shall judge all, according to all they knew; oh, and we alone know much. Your condemnation is just. 24Do you not know the Lamb of God did not merely die? No, but he died and prophesied that all the faithful would flee destruction. He died and showed the faith of John, his love for Mary. He died and honored God with his lips, sparing the Roman, and remembering the thief on the cross. 25And carrying your suffering and death that you would die in mere water and drink blood made true wine, you alone are asked to witness without nails in your wrists nor cross on your back. 26But I see even this is too much to ask. You ignore the acts of the apostles; therefore, when Christ comes again, slaughter him as you hired hands killed the witness of his apostle, emasculating yourselves as Paul so desired. 27May you end your revolting. 28May you submit to the governing authorities. 29May you rebuke the faithless brothers who wield the harlot's sword, which is rebellion. 30And may you redeem the lost as children of God. 31Whoever does not love does not know God, because God is love. 32Loving God, refuse the hypocrite their pride. 33"We know the scriptures," as does the devil, and he shudders as the demons shudder. 34To all who love the lost, as Christ first loved you, may the Father forgive the flock. 35God, they know not what they are doing; it is the shepherd who lied. But only remove the millstones from their necks. Amen.

IV Dan

[1]That God may strengthen your soul, having kept the faith, in accordance with the teachings of the saints, and if of the saints then of Jesus our Lord, who gave his Father's Spirit to the saints according to the will of God. Amen. [2]Having seen the evil of this world, the manifold sins hidden within even the saved, and the various lies the body is given over to, I find all joy in the few who remain steadfast, those who persevere, and all who do my Savior's will. [3]Many claim to know his will, and even to follow it, yet they refuse to bear fruit in keeping with the faith given by God; [4]and, having refused these deeds, they are without the faith of Abraham, holding to the fickle faith of demons, against which the brother of our dear Lord so earnestly warned. [5]But here, now, I write only to my brothers in faith, my sisters in love proved through silent sacrifice, having written already unto all in our body without ear, knowing that, in their pride, they will remain without works in keeping with righteousness, grieving the Spirit who wishes to work within them, that they would be brought into his Father's kingdom. Instead, God's name is blasphemed among the nations. Not for the sake of his righteous judgment, nor for the sake of unwavering justice—no, but for the foolishness, idiocy, and hypocrisy of our brothers before the promise of salvation. [6]Are you, then, in truth, one of these? Then submit yourself to the judgment, forgiveness, correction, and cleansing of Christ. [7]Having been cleansed yourself by the Spirit, would you deny these things from your fellow workers? And having shared the wisdom of his judgment, yourself judged, and seeing them refuse his judgment, themselves given the love of a fellow worker, would you side with the sin of their pride, or condemn their sin rightly in Christ that they might yet repent? [8]And this, then, is to pursue the way that Christ so earnestly walked, dividing in all speech and deed between truth and deceit, whether the deceit be among the saints, lying as a tare among the wheat, or among the lost, lying as a child among adults, unaware they speak insanities. [9]And we are all to pursue this truth in ourselves—yes, that even in our innermost thoughts the sword of Christ would judge and correct our intentions, keeping each thought in accord with righteousness. Should we see in our wisdom the shadows of evil, then as wisdom we will laugh at the wicked. Should we know in our hearts

covetousness, then we shall flee to Christ,
who saves wretched men. Should we see
the way of righteousness, having learned
truth, then we shall remain steadfast
through silence; for, having set the course,
our Lord can merely watch as we part the
waters. Amen. [10]And having accepted this
very sword, our mind—and if our mind
before Christ, so also our heart—shall be
given over to the will of God, as a man set
under authority. "Do this," yet will it be
done? As for myself, when my God says,
"Do this, and come, then go, and in all
run well, follow, never yet delay but ever
extend your will into mine," I find within
myself fear and trembling that I might
refuse, or fail, or be broken in my pursuit
of the Lord—he who keeps my soul that,
loving him, I cannot fail, and failing him,
I would know I had not loved, but only
loved being first loved, and my condemnation would be just. [11]Praise God, this joy
earned in faith, to know I have done his
will; love his teachings, to take pride in the
Father; and earn wages in keeping with
his kingdom. [12]And now, having earned
another mina, go, and come again with
yet more, so that our Father's kingdom
come, and will be done, as his will and
kingdom he has given to the Son, who
rose again and is the King of all, of even
the Father who promised he would give
all he has over to our Lord, and if all and
if the very Holy Spirit, then even himself,
to the Lamb who was slain. Amen. [13]Pray
ever to our Father, in the name of our
King. May all righteousness be found with
you, and may all blessings pour over the
saints on the last day, the day of judgment,
which we so patiently await.

V Dan

Chapter 1

[1]In light of the deception and corruption of the saints, as a saint, as a co-laborer in Christ Jesus my Lord, grace has been denied and peace obscured. Greetings. [2]To the Jews first and then to the gentiles, as was spoken in scripture before. But there is only the one, spoken to both Jew and gentile, and spoken to neither Jew nor gentile, for in Christ there is neither Jew nor gentile nor male nor female, but all are one; [3]all these come bound in the truth of scripture, yet all pervert scripture, if only as the Sanhedrin did before them. [4]Now, all scripture is written to the believers of the one true God: in times past, to the Jews and the believers therein—although all Jews were called to believe—[5]and in the age of the resurrection to all who believe, Jew or gentile, for believing there are still Jews in faith, and refusing to believe there are still Jews by right. Yes, to the Jew first, then also to the gentile, should either believe. [6]Thus, scripture written to the Jew was written to those who, in faith, were found also already in the knowledge of the scriptures of old, as known by Christ Jesus, who preached alone from and about these scriptures, as now itself recorded in scripture: Christ preaching out of the knowledge of the rituals of God, of the laws of God, of the history of God, and of the ways of God. [7]For even in this, without faith, the scriptures having been entrusted to the people of God, [8]the wellspring of knowledge of the writings of our God to his people, still being his people, are held sacred in the traditions of his people, if only that in their denial of his covenant they would heap coals into their own lap. Amen. [9]Thus, saying "to the gentiles" has been and ever was to those who were new in the knowledge of God, of his scriptures, and of those traditions by which we are to interpret the later writings, which change neither a jot nor a tittle of the writings given by God before, only recording the fulfilling of the will of God who prophesied, "I shall crush your head." [10]Were you, born into the assembly, raised in the wisdom of the scriptures, studied in the faith, in your arrogance, found reading "to the Jews" and thinking to yourself, "those godless fools," while reading "to the gentiles" while believing, "yes, for God now loves I"? [11]But God has ever loved all his children, asking little of some, and more of

the Jews, and now in Christ giving the Holy Spirit for strength to the greatest, the highest, yes, even the most of us, "to the Jew first and also to the gentile." 12You, then, are without excuse, all who, in knowledge of salvation scorn those apart from the light—you who pervert God's rebukes to the saints, instead declaring that God hated his own rituals, given to his people. 13"But we are free from these rituals, and are no longer bound to the sacrifice of Passover," as you would say, refusing to drink the blood of Passover in remembrance of our one Lamb who died for Adam, Isaac, Rahab, and the sins of the whole world. Amen. 14Or did Rahab not mark her window red as blood when her God passed over her and her household, although she was merely a daughter of God, that his promise of love would be fulfilled? 15And by what law did she do this work, a law of works, or a law of faith? Having the faith of her father Abraham 16made him her father by the love of God for the faithful, faith of Abraham in God, and love of righteousness as Rahab loved God escaping the things of this world. 17Not only do you refuse this same blood, and refuse to admit you are no more worthy of his manna than the flesh by which you were saved, but so also do you deny the washing by water. 18But let the washing of households be explained by the Jew first, then to the gentile, for this principle is right.

Chapter 2

1Now, then, you who eat curdled milk strained of a gnat, drenched with the dung of camels, you teachers of the gospel, you who gloss over the law—within which the prophets and the gospels are included—yes, you, trained by Gamaliel; were you not called to eat solid food? 2To the Hebrews, is this not in harmony with and written out of the knowledge of scripture? 3Yes, was this gospel of God promised beforehand out of holy scriptures, or did Paul through the Holy Spirit speak both "yes, yes" and "no, no"? 4Why, then, do you scorn the rituals of the Lord of the Sabbath? 5Why do you deny the God who is our one sacrifice participation is his death and resurrection? Is this sacrifice too simple? 6Why do you argue away the keeping of the faith, the guarding of the faith, the deeds, yes, even the works of this faith, the following unto death of this faith? 7Why do you deny that the Spirit spoke to Sapphira, that Judas was a saint and an apostle? 8When you promise that doubt is an illusion, you deny James, but James wrote to the Jews, and thus is lesser scripture. Yes, I know your heart! 9Understand the complex in light of the simple, then understand Romans in light of the parables of Christ, the faithful standards of Paul's profession before Agrippa, and reading all in light of the writings of Peter, read then also in light of the warning of Peter about the corruption of men such as yourselves, and repent, lest you

fall away. Yet how many already, having
scorned the Spirit, are twice dead? [10]Or
am I to cower before those who deny
the sovereignty of God to create sons?
[11]Am I to fear men who say, "God chose
to end my sins in part, and no sin in full,
and some only to restrain, that all saved
may fear in the end sins they no longer
may commit, and all who commit know,
'I was not saved, yet they should die as
I'"? [12]Am I to fear those who mock the
faith of the man who chose to say, "Lord,
remember me in your kingdom"? For
God alone chose that day to boast of his
kingdom. Did he then command that
a fool be brought up to heaven, having
confessed by command, to boast of this
boasting? [13]But search the scriptures and
you will find that it is the clay vessel that
became marred in the hands of the potter,
that he as God changed his intentions.
The potter Jeremiah watched, changing
his intentions for the pot, and God, being
refused by those he redeemed, changed his
intentions for those he labored over. [14]For
"there will be tribulation and distress for
every human being who does evil, the Jew
first and also the Greek, [15]but glory and
honor and peace for everyone who does
good, the Jew first and also the Greek.
[16]For God shows no partiality." [17]And one
must ask, if this is to twist the scriptures,
by what measure is scripture found right?

Chapter 3

[1]Thus, having knowledge of the rituals
of the Son of God, in light of the rituals
given to the Jews alone by the son of God,
knowing that no sacrifice may save, for
"your hands are drenched in the blood
of the innocent," [2]it is by sacrifice we are
saved, for Christ died as our one sacrifice
that all who would believe and be free
from doubt, having faith with works,
would be as safe in God's hands as the thief
who declared in faith the depths of sin and
glory of the Lord he failed to serve, as the
Syrian who baptized in the Jordan, as the
Shepherd who repented having slaugh-
tered a man for his one sheep, as the apostle who thrice denied our Lord, and as the
persecutor who in pride of knowledge of
the faith approved the murder of a saint,
for all in faith were forgiven their sin and
deception just as Abraham the father of
our faith was forgiven his twice handing
over of Sarah. [3]Without repentance there
is no forgiveness, without love there is
no grace, and without obedience all shall
die without mercy. Amen. [4]In this way
we are all to follow the Son of God who
preached peace, who sacrificed all, who
shared life and resurrected even the truth,
unto the gates of his kingdom, given to
him by his father, and into all eternity,
should we repent. [5]Yes, having been born
into the knowledge of the truth, drawing
closer in knowledge, and joining deeper
into the assembly, you call this knowledge faith; [6]yet without repentance and

sacrifice, obedience and the Spirit, and the
handing over of the flesh to the new heart,
dying to the self as to finish a race, none
are saved—no, not even one. 7For a tower
left unfinished, a tower built without the
cornerstone, a tower set without its foundation, and a tower made whole of three
minas, "and here, see Peter, we used all
five," is a work of the deceived and the
deceiver. 8But all who build in integrity,
never lying before God, who indwells
with the saint and hears all even through
the conscience, shall be forgiven their
sins. 9For none build rightly, yet many
as shrewd managers defraud God, serving as wolves who preach "peace, peace"
to goats. 10Yes, and none build rightly,
yet the few build a tower worthy of their
God. 11Knowing they are unworthy,
knowing there is blood on their hands, yet
loving their God, they build so that their
body—yes, even their dead flesh—may be
a worthy house for our God, a worthy
temple to our Father's Spirit. 12And thus
he says, "And your house and your kingdom shall be made sure forever before me.
Your throne shall be established forever."
13Or is this not the love the Son of David
had for David before? 14Now go, do deeds
in keeping with righteousness, that our
King would see you kept in the faith of
the salvation of the gospel. 15And know
now that here lies the blade which emas-
culated the heresy of Augustine, yes, may
sola fide remain ever only the corruption
and denial of James, who the Protestant
hated. 16Praise Jesus my Lord, the Son of
the Father, who gives faith to the faithful, who loves his sons, who will damn
the enemies of his son, who gave his own
Spirit unto his son, giving Christ rule over
all, given even a throne higher than the
throne of his reign before his conquering
of death, yes, the very throne of God, who
would not deny the son whom he loves.
Grace and peace, amen.

VI Dan

Chapter 1

1Finally and again, Dan, of the one faith,
yes, in which you all share, although
my rebuke is heavy and my wrath at
your lack of deeds waxes great, a fellow
worker, to all who would hear, as I tire
of all who ought to listen, let us close.
2I find I need to speak only these six in
this manner. 3The learned know that the
saints of our storied church wrote each
other and the flock often in this way,
for what is an epistle but a letter to be
read, and what else will saints ever share
between themselves but thoughts on the
faith and rebukes of the faithful, for the
faithful shall find their praise in God. 4Oh
yes, but of course I need first confess my
opening declarations, in knowledge—for
who can pen faith itself—that I share the
right knowledge of the God of our faith.
But allow that I now begin in earnest the
first confession. 5Before heaven and earth
was our God. 6Creating alone heaven and
earth was our God, although wisdom
watched, as the sayings testify. 7And still
our God was not alone, yes, for with God
was God his Son. 8And with God was God
his breath, who is all life, for God is life.
9And with the Spirit and the Son eternally
was their Father—thus is our one God, for
God is one. 10All created was created by
God; nothing uncreated exists save our
God, who himself created—yes, and eternally God was kept with God, for by God,
God is one. 11Then, having created, God
created also sons, 12and having created sons
created a son to be the father of sons, and
daughters, and one day, the day having
now been fulfilled, by his sons the Son of
God would be made a son of God that the
Son of God could fulfill the creation of all
sons of God in the hope of a new heaven
and a new earth, 13this first heaven hosting
fallen angels just as this first earth hosted
fallen sons, all to be washed away with fire,
and many having first been washed away
by death, and by water. Amen. 14All this
is recorded only in the writings given by
God, as little is known save what the Lord
shared openly. Although many received
visions, they each testified only to what
they were given as set under authority to
share, 15for no prophet speaks of himself
but only in accordance with the Holy
Spirit, who is God given over by God to
the Son of God, the Spirit's being handed
over made right as the Son was established
by God as King over all, all having been

handed over to our one Lord Christ Jesus in fulfillment of faith and love through his death and resurrection, to which all the saints will attest. [16]And having been given the Holy Spirit that all his sons would be baptized both in water by repentance, and in fire by the laying on of hands, as the holy oil before, the body is brought into Christ by the Spirit who is God in this life, that even in this life, in this groaning world, the word would be known and the gospel shared to all the corners of the earth. Amen. [17]That upon his return the saints will find themselves prepared for their King, who is alone King, for our King has declared the Captain of the Host King over all as his promised reward for his sacrifice, both for the lost and for the Father who desired that the lost would be saved, sending the Son according to prophecy, as recorded throughout history and fulfilled according to his will, conquering death and hades. Amen. [18]It is in light of this judgment, and of his books, which shall be read on the last day, that all are called to keep their conscience clear before God and man, as the apostle and saint who is our brother, Paul, so confessed. [19]And now, having spoken from beginning to end, let us begin in earnest. [20]How many may say, "I spoke in all strength, in the wisdom of our saints before God, in light of the scriptures and their Spirit-guided interpretation, with all words of truth; how holy it is, how holy it was, yes, each word chosen out of faith, and all right teaching," and yet still those clanging gongs without love, without deed, go only to hell? [21]As Paul warned, faith without love is dead. [22]As James said, faith without works is dead. [23]And as all know, faith is worked out through love, for to deny a cold brother clothes, yet offer prayer, is not love, although it may be faith. [24]Now who would scorn John, for "whoever does not love does not know God, because God is love." [25]Yes, whoever does not love does indeed abide in death, and this is said of the saints. [26]Thus, even though you all reek of this dying faith, I know our God called you, called you by saving faith and the seal of salvation, which is yet perfect, as was Sapphira's. [27]And having been called, having been redeemed, having been set free, you have not obeyed.

Chapter 2

[1]Christ died for all, and here already we have lost all who will never agree with the light of scripture, having their own light, higher than scripture—for scripture may be read plainly by mere fishermen—yet they are true Pharisees, [2]and having died for all, all rebelled. [3]Yes, God's son was sacrificed, and you make no sacrifice. [4]You were asked to do well. Instead, you fail, confident you will be named "good and faithful servant." [5]Do well or fall away as Judas. And do you now tremble, or deny that Judas fell? You and I cannot both be right, and yet I read rightly all scripture, not only those lies which tickle my arrogance and cowardice, as you feel

confident for twisting into sin the righteous riddles which were given to guard the mind from thoughts of damnation. Yet have you guarded your faith? Then so shall your heart ever falter in the truth you name doubt. [6]God owes you nothing, but saves who he wills: all who choose to do his will. [7]It is for this reason I hate you, you of the church, and of the churches, and of the saints without the body, and of the blood, with children unclean; by water they are to be made holy, as all are then to be made sons of fire by the anointing by fire. Yes, none have escaped my notice. [8]For just as knowledge of faith shall not save, so shall knowledge of loving deeds not save, save unless they are done by love. [9]In this all have made a mockery of Christ Jesus our Lord. And still, you all boast. [10]Do you not know that Christ, even in your rebellion, is still by your faith your Lord, and that by the faith of Abraham, who took blade to slay Isaac, serving the Son by the Spirit of love as the Father commands, you shall be saved in Christ—who will say to those that know him, which is faith, but dishonor him, which is not love, "I never knew you"? [11]Yes, our one God will condemn you to hell unless you repent. And how few are twice dead to be without hope, and thus are without excuse. [12]You are unlike the twice dead, who are without excuse, without hope, without faith, and who speak intelligently of the nature of theology, having lost the very Breath of God. [13]For we, where there are yet any in true faith, bold faith, to speak of, of this faith in the God of our God, yes, we shall not profane Jesus, who worshipped God, nor the Father, by denying he is God over God. [14]Only study the scriptures and remember these things are old, not new, although your heart is lazy and your mind is hard (but who has heard of a lazy heart, and of what concern is your mind to the things of faith?). [15]Oh you of hardened heart! [16]Cannot you see the bold faith of the few, which seeks to be hidden but shines on a hill? Which seeks to roar like the lion and yet is warm as the wool of the lamb? [17]I write of my poverty, yet this is my wealth. I write of my vast wealth, and am paid only in stray minas. Of what worth is the one to the ten? That the one had only made one, and kept two. But no, no! Go out and fail our Messiah that I would prosper. And how many levy such a claim as this against our God? [18]Yes, the bold in faith, being kind and simply subtle, as to put you to shame, you lean on in need and reject in joy. [19]Or did you believe that God did not see into your heart, which he built for you? Where he records all you do, that it would be known and made right, if only you would repent? [20]The harvest nears, yet you were content to worship the idols of the heart of the chaff, called theology—yet it is only made theology in name. [21]And here is a test: which is true theology, that God is love, that God is hate, or that God is beyond such things? Yet God is love, God does hate, and thus he is not above a righteous heart, but weeps over Jerusalem and Lazareth. And in this we then see how the God of man is a man, and

shares in the affections of the God of God,
who is our Father, whose image is the Son;
therefore, the love and hate of a son for a
mother, a friend for his friends, a teacher
for his students, a great teacher for those
who call him great, a Jew for the gentile, a
Jew for the Jew, a man for all women, are
not Christ's alone but an inheritance from
the Father. 22But what heir is not all and
more than his Father, such that to be less
than his Father, when chosen by his Father,
would be a failing of a Father or of a Son
made perfect heir? 23And here I close. For
I say, "The Father elevates the Son above
himself," and you tremble. And, "The Son's
humanity is not his but his Father's who
shares all with his Son, having made man
but in their image, which is the Father's,
given to the Son," and you scoff, "Christ
is a worm like us now; the Father is pure."
24Christ is no worm, but you are no sons;
you have failed in your humanity, and are
by choice dying in the mud. And yet sons
you were created and as sons you shall
perish, without inheritance, or love, being
hated, for you chose hate. 25But choose love,
choose truth, choose the way, follow the
path laid by your conscience, which you
strive to keep clear before God and man, for
your conscience is not yours—what do you
know of wisdom and righteousness?—but is
the Holy Spirit who is God, rebuking and
at times even defending you. 26You deny
even this? But this was Paul …

About the Author

DAN DAVID ELIHU, born Jacob Anglin, was raised by a Protestant home-schooling family in northern Virginia. He decided to become an author after he became aware of the American Gospel documentaries and thoroughly disagreed with their theology. Currently twenty-six, he began writing at the age of twenty-three. This personal obsession led to the Death of Protestant Theology project, and a desire for the body to be unified into the will of Christ. His favorite secular authors are F. Scott Fitzgerald, Friedrich Nietzsche, George Orwell, Christopher Hitchens, Frank Herbert, and Thomas Jefferson. He heralds C.S. Lewis, in all of his writing, especially in the most terrifying and thoroughly deemed questionable, as God's greatest saint. 1 John 4:8, the thief on the cross, and the book of Job are his three favorite places in scripture.

www.ingramcontent.com/pod-product-compliance
Lightning Source LLC
LaVergne TN
LVHW090538110826
845146LV00003B/1165

* 9 7 9 8 2 3 4 0 5 2 4 5 2 *